Forever Love

IN VOLUMES

Forever Love in Volumes
All Rights Reserved.
Copyright © 2022 Aken Vivian Wariebi
v3.0

This is a work of poeticized fiction. The opinions expressed in this manuscript are solely the opinions of the author and do not represent the opinions or thoughts of the publisher. The author has represented and warranted full ownership and/or legal right to publish all the materials in this book.

This book may not be reproduced, transmitted, or stored in whole or in part by any means, including graphic, electronic, or mechanical without the express written consent of the publisher except in the case of brief quotations embodied in critical articles and reviews.

I-Can Works

ISBN: 978-0-9707503-2-7

Library of Congress Control Number: 2022917027

Cover Photo © 2022 Phil M. Merriam. All rights reserved - used with permission.

PRINTED IN THE UNITED STATES OF AMERICA

Other books by Aken V. Wariebi

Think as your heart beats

Living Through Poetry

Contents

ACKNOWLEDGMENT

FOREWORD

PROLOGUE: Personal Quotations from the Author (I)

REFLECTIONS ....Pages 1–20

FROM MY LENS ....Pages 21-52

THOUGHTS TO PONDER OVER-...............Pages 53-99

JUST SOME RANDOM THOUGHTS.......Pages 101–143

EPILOGUE: Personal Quotations from the Author (II)

NOTES

Acknowledgment

First, I would like to thank God for allowing me to keep on writing despite whatever odds come my way. Now, I know and fully understand the verse in God's word better, that states, "I can do all things through Christ who strengthens me." (Philippians, 4:13)

I had the pleasure and privilege of working with kids called "At-risks." I never knew that I would meet kids who had so much to give me, far more than I could ever give them. Their resilience as survivors amazed me each day. They yearn for one thing, "love." However, for them, love seemed scarce, and yet I, in my wildest dreams, could never have imagined that I had so much love to give. I thought I was planting a seed to provide skills in whatever aspect as needed in their lives. But I got taught instead about the lessons of genuine love, the value it has, and what that gives in all our lives. The messages that we interpret from love and not just by how we express it, but also how we react to it, all of it, in its entirety.

I worked with these kids, mostly in the Eastern part of The United States of America. I realized one of my dreams, working with the youth, come true. I initiated many working sessions explicitly piloted for homeless and runaway youth. They liked to call our groups interactions "workshops." I wrote these poems from those moments. I always told the kids at night, at least the ones I saw before they retire for the night or before I went home, mostly the most recent kids, I said, "Forever Love." They asked me often the meaning of those words. I told them it meant, "You are loved forever and love yourself forever." Yes, they sometimes got on my last nerve, but I still cared.

I got to experience kids from diverse backgrounds, mindsets, lifestyles, and ethnicities. They have a lot to teach us collectively and individually. All of them can teach us, today's adults, much more than we think they can or care to admit. Only if and when we are willing and eager to listen. We, as a society, can teach each other if only we first are willing to learn. I want to thank every kid in the USA that has crossed my path with the label "At-Risk." Thank you for letting me see you as you are. Your tenacity, strength, and willingness to cope through the unimaginable make you, my inspiration. No, not your faults or weakness, nor your "bad" as we all have those; some of us just hide it so. But for your strength and what it teaches people about humanity. Blessings and peace to you all now and always! I wish you all the best in all your endeavors.

I, however, must thank a few others who contributed to making this book possible. They are, my former co-worker Mrs. Tanisha Gamble Snead who suggested this idea; my editors, who were patient with me throughout the process; my publisher for working with me; and those who took the time to give reviews and critique my work. To all of you, the two words of "Thank you" does not seem enough, yet they are the two words that I can give right now. My thanks also go to Dr. Anthony Barclay, who wrote the foreword. My book designer Mr. Phillip Merriam. Thank you all for being on the journey of putting this project in print and to completion. May you too be blessed always. To those friends who let me just go on in conversation about anything and everything and still stand by my side, I say thanks to you too. My boring conversations you tolerate so well. Please know I am here for you as well.

Thanks to all my teachers in Monrovia, Liberia, West Africa, my professors everywhere who saw me and accepted me as I am, and those who helped mold me to be who I am becoming. Now, I know how difficult that job can be. The foundation I received in education was well worth it. I agree with the adage, it takes a village to raise a child; I mean this literally. It is a teamwork effort and a very challenging job.

To my parents and others who have gone before me, I also say thank you. I promise that I will keep writing as there is so much to write about. I find Poetry a kind of literature that I can best convey my stories as all stories need to be told in any way possible. We breathe our words, and we transform them into stories from which we can learn. I believe that these stories can help to bring change to society; good change. We cannot ever get tired of telling stories because life will not ever get tired of evolving. Generations can and will be healed if and only if our stories are told.

Foreword

Forever Love In Volumes by Aken Vivian Wariebi is a remarkable anthology of poems, innovatively accompanied by personal quotes at the beginning and end of the book appropriately called Prologue: Personal Quotations from the Author (I) and Epilogue: Personal Quotations from the Author (II). I, a published poet and author of other non-fiction publications, appreciate this anthology and applaud the author for her skills, dedication, and perseverance in producing it.

The book seems to build on the thematic flavor of love, appreciation, and various attributes of humanity articulated in some of her other works including, Twenty-Five Years of Bliss (a dedicatory 25th wedding anniversary poem for her sister and brother-in-law) written in 2006 and Living Through Poetry, published in 2013.

The author employs a tapestry of poetic styles and rhythms. It includes enjambed lines and a mixture of rhyming and free verses. I consider the book a poetic exposition of love and humanity's virtues and vices. It is also sprinkled with religious sentiments, subtle references to racial and political issues, and related matters that people encounter in their daily lives.

The love themes in some of the poems resonate with me. I was particularly touched by the author's interaction with the "At Risks" kids from which her motivation to write this book evolved. The poems, titled You Matter and Forever Love, eloquently articulates the kids' self-worthiness, their capacity to love and be loved, as well as, their inherent potential to contribute to and benefit from the world today. I believe these poems set the tone that follows in many of the other verses about love and life's concerns.

In general, the book is magnificently crafted. The coverage of the experience of losing a parent and a cherished parental legacy; medical concerns of a loved one; unfulfilled romantic relationship; and people's general attitude and behavior are profound. The expressed sentiments on these issues and others are universal and unbounded by time. Some of the messages conveyed are straightforward; others are more subtle. Overall, they reflect human realities. This book will prove to be one that keeps the readers captivated.

Anthony Barclay, PhD
(yalcrab77@yahoo.com)
Author of:
*Personal Human Decency: The PHD from the University of Life (Xlibris, 2011)
*Coming Together: The Ins and Outs of Liberia Ups and Downs (Xlibris, 2020)

PROLOGUE: Personal Quotations from the Author (I)

- Your enemies are close but keep in mind that God is a much more intimate force than the enemy will ever be.
- It is not always about what they can do for you, but mostly how they treat you that should count.
- It is no love and never was, if you wish the person, you love not to be happy. You MUST mean and wish happiness and well-being, even if you are not in the mix.
- Not everyone in your life belongs in every chapter of it
- Life usually gives you a reason to reinvent yourself, make it a positive one ---it is called growth!
- Love yourself so immensely that loving people comes naturally!
- Be your best to do your best, remembering though that sometimes your best comes as a result of your worst.
- Being grateful for everything includes especially the small things, because sometimes the big things come with its own price tag.
- If we have joy in our hearts, it is only our mission to spread it and leave it on others, not only like a butterfly's touch but with an impact that will last a lifetime.
- See yourself as a candle and don't limit or dim the light that God has given you. Recognize it, embrace it, and let it shine. It is there deep inside of you, discover it, explore it, claim it and spread it!
- Age does not seem to matter in maturity or immaturity. Maturity MAY come with experience. However, Immaturity may come with ignorance, lack of exposure and much more.
- Observe and declare, remembering actions speak far better than words ever will.

In living life, I've learned, if we continue or choose to look at the flaws of ourselves and others, we miss the richness of the entire experience of living including; it's worth, it's value and its essence. In so doing, there is no growth. But with the awareness of viewing and accepting the strengths and abilities, all parties gain so much more and so life goes...and growth continues

- When the Lord leads us, all we need to do is follow. When he moves us, it is for the better?
- People watch you especially when you are not paying attention and even when you are. God, watches however, in the light and dark
- Appreciate God, he has time for you and always will no matter what. With man, consider he who frees his time for you not who only has time for you in your presence or when they hear from you
- There is power in ignorance just as much as there is power in knowledge.
- Silence is not only violence, it is abuse. The silent with knowledge is just as evil as the doer with action. If we are silent when we have any vital information that can free the oppressed, we ourselves are no different than the oppressors.
- Turning off someone else's light won't make your problems disappear. In fact, your problems may just be a little more. So, trust not man, but God and your burden will be lighter. Build yourself up and in so doing others will not be destroyed but lifted up
- Some only know how to take. Some only know how to give. What matters from the heart is the love. Where is the love in this matter?

REFLECTIONS

Standing because life is still beautiful,
the world is still with changes.
Hurts come and go, fields dry up,
dreams are born yet constantly.
Hope meets and greets, never totally fading away.
We hold on uncontrollably,
expecting not as much as we think.
Finding our way, coping and embracing,
the good, bad and the ugly
unconsciously.

Aken Vivian Wariebi

YOU MATTER

As life was breathed into you, it began
Your value, your worthiness
Your presence of which some depend
As important as life is, as it deepens
It defines you in miracles, not dollars and cents

You better believe that you are a miracle
One of grace, given grace to one day ascend
But for now, put on earth to represent
A force so much greater than man
You must know that you too, matter

Know and believe it; it is true
You matter far more than you ever knew
Claim your vigor and your power
Never think that others need to pay the rent for you

You mattered before you arrived
And being here shouldn't make you feel curious
You are from a valuable gem
This is, in fact, serious
The creator makes no mistakes
That can be recalled to fend

So, remember, you matter
each and every day to the end
If birds, pigs, and flies' matter
Their places on earth never negotiable
What about you, my dear friend?

With God, all things are possible.

I say to you feel the dream and reality
That God ordained that is you
There is no partiality in the formation of this actuality
Then you will see, you will not need
To gather any evidence on rows while entering the penitentiary
No matter whoever you are or where you are from, please be sure
You matter

And you'll eventually realize that
God never closed that door
The one with hatred and guile, instead he made love refined
So here are two words to recite to erase the devil's lies
"YOU MATTER"
No matter who or what attempts to interrupt
This, I hope you'll soon discover
You matter, keep sticking to it,
for that is the core of the matter

FOREVER LOVE

Staring in nowhere
Nothing appears
But love
deep inside
Spreading on
The outside of me
spilling over sloppily
With me in between
Calmly calculating
This feeling
That I can't explain
That you bring
And I grow
inside of me
To share, multiply, and I fantasize
running wild, with ecstasy
slowly never rehearsing
the place, the space, the source
can't emulate
nor translate
I'm on fire and have no pacifier
Free to express, free to impress
Simply free to own it, claim it,
FOREVER
emancipate,
love forever,
forever love,
through eternity
Mental slavery
Not the destiny

This Poem was inspired by each and every kid that I have worked with in my career, I call them, " God's Precious Jewels" as we all really are, but society calls them "At-Risk Youth." This poem and this book are from my prospective working with kids and mine alone.

The struggles continue…

BEING DIFFERENT

For future reference
We are all unique
In many respects
Our uniqueness spells
Our core, our character
Our style, our views
Our opinions, Our utilization of
Common sense

For future reference
We are who we are
Created as one
An individual
Collectively fighting a cause

Arguing a point, struggling...
Being silent, talking, protesting within or without,
loyalty, commitment, obligation, unification, separation,
Near or far, gifted

For future reference we stare, ignoring, reacting, acting, embracing
Performing, entertaining, praying, laughing, stalling, thinking, hugging,
Doing all of this by choice
In our own way, with our own signature, making our own legacy

Perhaps being different
We expand, soar or stand still

Not moving, only learning how to define ourselves
Crawling into our own reality, accepting if we let go
But knowing growth is beaming within,
with the potential that different isn't
better, it is "best" in our terms

DON'T LET GO

Don't let go of the calm within your soul
Nor the smile on your face
Nor the love in your heart
Retain the hope that lets you go
Wherever you are thrown
When life wears you down
And you fall in between

Don't let go of the peace you have within
Nor the solemnness you feel
Nor the dreams you hold so dear
Your time will come to shine
The stage is but so wide
The rain never lasts a lifetime
Nor does evil always revive
Hold on to something stronger

Don't you lose your sight on the unimportant
The significant remains
But live the life of a king or queen
Yell, but pray if you please
Grasp that which your mind consumes
Know to throw out the bad and let the good remain
Improve while attempting to be what you want to become
Only if you know it is what is the best for you

NEVER FORGET

Never forgot the bridge that crossed you
Not necessarily the one that broke you down
Just never forget to remember who walked with you
Through your next chapter or perhaps to it as you shine
To the goals of your kind
That suits your ambition

In building yourself, never forget the foundation
    on which you stand
Its construction was not built by you alone
In fact, it was not built merely by human hands
Those skillful hands that acted the part
They may not have been your friends

But perhaps, just perhaps it was why your paths cross
Just for that temporary stay
Maybe it never was a lifetime thing, that person
Or those persons in between

In growing, we must move on indeed
But our reflection must spell something
    that we can be proud off
Not only what we do for others
But what others have done for us

How we treat each other, after the fact, spells and says a lot
It provides a lot to comprehend, a lot not only
    about our character
Mostly about us inwardly, truly we know each other better
Our helpers and ourselves, even if we grow apart

Not from our initial meeting
But from the ending of that which we find and seek for closure
So, we never forget the reflection we see
And how it makes us feel

With a smile or a frown, whether one or both may come to our minds
But we must never forget the purpose for which our bridge was built
And never lose sight of our reminders of our true friends and
Our permanent enemies

WE APPRECIATE YOU!

To give of your own free time is generous
It is a sign of compassion
It is indeed a sign of your quality
Because time is precious
In a way, time is the essence of humanity
of our very lives, of the human race

So, when you give your time
It shows and spells out your uniqueness
When you give it freely?
It is admirable
Many can't do that

There is no way of pretending to give your time
You either give it or you don't
It can't be haphazard, it usually never is
One thing is for sure
It is a blessing, a sacrifice
A form of selflessness

It is a loving feeling to be
To become and remain what we refer to as a volunteer
The gratitude you may never hear or see nor even imagine
You do lend your wings for others to soar
And yes, you touch lives

You do reflect goodness and positivity
Just because, simply because, you are you
It is unanimously empowering
And we want you to know

We appreciate you!
Keep shining, we thank you!

OUR SECRETS

Burdened by the weight that we carry because of it
The shame that we think is attached to it
People's opinions and views if and when we reveal
We not only use a mask but sometimes a far deeper cover
A kind of blanket of a darker color
that may hide it even from ourselves

That way, we can decide that it isn't even there
And wear a smile, living a life as if all is aright
Sometimes we reach for greatness, we hope to
Find some peaceful medium,
perhaps becoming a comedian,
Or even a far more serious profession
fitting in exactly right, after a lot of practice

Our demeanor may constantly change,
depending on our audience
The situation, or various circumstances
or consequences
We then dream of two things:

The day we can reveal or the time
we wish that our secrets leave no stain
And perhaps disappear, so we hide it so well
But it may be at others expense while others'
behaviors make our secrets so discreet
But it all just depends

Somehow, we live through others' trials and
tribulations with or without support
We may cope with cheers from

those we determine as family
It is all a waiting game for the conclusion
to our stories, not necessarily the ending
But we last sometimes out of curiosity
if we are lucky or better, yet blessed.

ACCUSED

Now how on earth
can I survive
The accusations?
You lie before me
Because of my race and
all of my taste
I flaw in awe of your guilt
accusing me of your assumed fate
Oh, how in shock
I am of your assumptions
Your stereotypical accusations
calling them options

And my reactions? I cry at night
sometimes and think
Because I am who I am and
what I am meant to be

Yes, I can be grand,
if only you admit your functions
But when you misrepresent me
I have the courage to climb
and surprise me

I am free, and I can tell you
For you, it means nothing
For me, I rise often

WHAT IF IT WAS LOVE

What if it was love
Not abuse or jinx
Just genuine taste
That you didn't see

You didn't know me, nor my love
You had not experienced such
T'was foreign to you but also to me
Your spirit was strong, so I stood aside
In awe of you and your beauty

What if it wasn't as you thought?
I must apologize
That you misread but then again
Then again
Misunderstandings are
possible being, in love

KIND EYES

Those eyes that see
Yet don't capture and behold
Embrace and accept no flaws,
no judgment, and no wrongs

Those eyes that see the hidden,
the gems that shine within
Those gifts your talents and skills
The potential that many can't recognize
Because for them they're pesticides

Those eyes that stare deeply,
far deeper than most
Finding the positive details in you
Kind eyes blue or black or
brown perhaps a different shade

Finding in you and me the lost,
the scars, the truth
Those eyes that see the
strength yet burying you
but not in your weakness
Nor circumstance

But sparingly selecting and
anticipating the good,
acknowledging the part of you
The best part that
everyone else keeps missing

DON'T CHANGE YOUR GOOD

Even if there is stormy weather
Don't change the way you find the stars
Don't change, and if your friends laugh; just smile
Don't change the walk on a five-mile line, nor the color of your eyes
Don't change; the road is too long
Although you are tired, we'll still sing your song

For as we gage our styles don't hide for too long
Wise guy
Just don't change who you are
For now, even if you change your mind's lies
or are they truths based on bribes?
I've missed your twirl on the dance floor
Where I imagine you in my arms

I've missed your smile, your sunshine fire
I've really missed you, or have I?
I wonder if you'll change when you realize
The joke was on me!
Now smile pretty woman,
Imagine me as your handsome young guy!

FIND ME

Today, I search far and wide
For something and I'm not sure why
Frankly, I don't know quite yet
What I'm looking for

Today, I search far and wide
Today, I cried
Because you didn't have to do what you did
But you did and I'm glad

Today I search for something
Nothing seems to matter
Yet I had to climb a ladder
Falling every hour
Struggling and not regretting the cry
Now I know why

A WOMAN'S HEART

In walking the halls of life
We meet women of all types
The ones we never thank
The ones who always mean well
The ones who get us in a lot of mess
The ones who drive us insane

And the ones who are interested
in our well-being
Not every woman is the same
But we need to thank women
Because one never knows
what a woman heart means
Nor what it holds

IT DOESN'T MATTER

It doesn't matter what I do; they steal
My joy, my peace, I want to hide
They steal my mind if they have to
In order to shine then leave
They've done it all my life
They make a living off me
That is how they survive

With poor taste; I can't cry
Because the lid is open yet I don't fly
it doesn't matter what happens
They'll do it till I die
the fact is, it isn't family ties
What it is, is abuse on all sides

FROM MY LENS

THERE IS STRENGTH IN EACH OF OUR STORIES,
IF ONLY WE TRY TO SEE IT.
IF AND WHEN WE DO, WE'LL ALSO SEE
LOVE, PEACE, HOPE AND COURAGE SOMEWHERE.

AKEN VIVIAN WARIEBI

THE ESSENCE OF KINDNESS

A brand one may want
 to have exposed
Yes, a brand all it's own
I'd have to say it spreads
the world over like swells
on the ocean's surface

Kindness can't be bought nor sold
Just extended or spread
Or scattered on oars
Peeling as easily and carefully
from its source

The essence and originality
Teaches wisdom, especially
Love steps in, out of curiosity
Fire burns dangerously
In it's peak blooming
Deeply
Beautifully sending peace,
no matter the loads

CRY NO MORE

Cleverly calculate the peace,
 the happiness
The feelings of worthiness
Calculate the odds of negotiation
With your emotion; all of them

The contribution of your choices
to express anger,
Sadness and pain, or happiness,
 joys, sorrows, feelings of blame
Cry no more though soldiers

Let your strength say so
You can handle more than you know
Remember, God won't give you what you can't handle
So, value your tears as gold
You win because God says so

FULLY COVERED

With ashes as damaged goods
With lead on top of the view
With fertilizer doing its job
I suppose
The living has good luck, up and through

With fearlessness apparent
and casual flaws exposed
And tumbling blocks, a way to soar
And having on temporary clothes
To listen to fault finders
And have the greed to live
And begin again as others would
And learn of experiences told

With flashy brand-name clothes
And casual jobs to roar
With failures, so many
they don't decompose
while living on death's row

I am fully covered
No matter how the picture looks
Deep inside and externally
I do believe because I am
permanently engraved and
I am in my heavenly father's book

THE UGLY SIDE

Well, the face doesn't
tell the entire story
Nor the car I drive
Nor the school I went to
My career has nothing to show
but the money I've earned,
albeit slow

My grade point average
My elevated calamities
My human nature fatalities
And so much more

That ugly side of me
may hide today at most
But, it can only be buried
and covered for so long like a sore

But then I have to let go
some see me as an angel
Some as a threat or so
My ugly side never tells a lie, though
I'm just saying, Let the truth be told

GOODNESS

It is shown in ways we can't
understand but appreciate
We stand grateful and in awe
We get support from unknown sources
As if our blessings conquer all

We may have negativity
But it runs far away
When goodness appears
And yes, within all of us
There is a level of evil
But let's not argue
About the percentage

The challenges may sometimes go
or may stay a little longer
Then what do we want to pay homage to?
But the lessons in goodness doesn't share a
tear but dresses up in smiles
Wearing it from ear to ear

Goodness sends positive energy
in all the right spaces
and places can never misinterpret
But all along through life's walkway
We see it lurking in our hearts,
secret phases on fences

LOOK AROUND

There is much to see
To feel
To appreciate
Much to love
And be confused about
For questions to come
And answers have a field day

There is much to create
To discover
To recognize
And believe
To validate
To collaborate
To hold on to
only if you can

Look around
To embrace
To accept
To ignore
or regret

Look around you
A lot of gifts
A lot of opportunities
A lot of noise
Peace
But mostly, a lot of miracles
And you are one of them

INHALE THE FUTURE

The past is gone
Let it go
you've been there, lived there
Your failures, you ask?
it's okay...learn
Your mistakes, you say?
Do the same...
There are lessons to be learned
You are a student
When these occur
Don't worry, your turn will come to teach
That is the purpose of living

The present is now
A clean page
Like a sheet of spotless snow
Another chance for you
For all of us
Who have made it thus far
You are not alone
In this and never will you be
Relax and chill
Don't sweat it
Know it
It's true
That is the purpose of living

The future is yonder
Somewhere far but really near
Maybe sitting in your heart right now
you stand close to it

Real close
It matters to inhale it
Slowly, gradually
Because it comes usually unexpected
Undenied
Believe
Inhale the future in your time
your way, your choice for your stay
It is alright; you just did
Breathe

NEVER LET IT CONQUER

Refuse its entrance
Never allow it
Do not open the door
for negativity
Drama of nonsense
Frivolous is what it is
Bring about toss points to negate
Not divert, nor redirect
Not peace nor contentment
Let it not conquer
That which could weigh you down
Run, keep running the race of positivity
Keep on no matter what it takes
you can handle it

EXHALE THE PAST

Open your mouth
Blow it out
All of it from your gut
Your mind
and Soul
Let your heart follow
if only for a moment
Until the past disappears
As your heart would walk it halfway
Then say goodbye
And hello to now and tomorrow

Release the pain
The rawness of it
has to go along with its core
All of it needs to flow
Far away from you soon
Keep it simple

Blow
Send it far away
Walk away
Run away
Stay away
Exhale
It is gone for the love of life
Keep it there

Wow, don't we have to learn
Trusting isn't so easy
Experience teaches that

But life, wow!
So many detours
Twists and turns

Love and hate
And a whole lot more
In all forms and fashions
On all kinds of corners
Hidden in the dark
Folded in imaginations

But right now, is the opportunity
Allowed for it, all of it to sink in
And then the journey
Begins of reasoning
The process...well
Wow...the facts and fictions
In between years may go by
Or days or months or centuries
and leaving may never come naturally

MESSAGES

When messages are sent
We may hear but not listen
Sense but not feel
Wonder but not question
Soar but not leap

We may run or walk slowly
Love creating hate
We may fall never staying
Down too long and avoid a hit
Stumbling as we crawl

Yet, we may deny it all

We may write without pondering
Judge without knowing
Laugh without smiling
Only to reply to nothing

We may leave without entering
Yell without screaming
Plant but without sowing
Act without meaning

Messages do that all the time
So we pay attention only
Sometimes without caring

PERFECT COLLISION

Well, like perfect timing
The details matter?
Or do they hide themselves?
Predicting, elevator style?
A collision, timely
Brings about what kind of explanation?
What kinds of mystery?
In the imperfections of perfection?

BALANCE

Busy as a bee
As an elephant
What affects the most?

Finding that balance
That little moment
To straighten out
To have the scale

Swaying slowly or
Not at all; never come,
and then what?

I'll have to think about it

Swift talkers
Slow thinkers
Never ever say this
Nor realizes it

Game changers don't either
But they tell themselves
In the thought process

Many wonder why some
Make a nice life
while others don't
Many only wonder thinking hard
Not doing enough

Some bypass thinking

All together
But complain
And pull down others
Some lift up others
Forgetting themselves

Well as for me
Let me tell you something
Well, this is the truth
I didn't forget
I'll just have to think about it

KNOW WHAT TIME IT IS

The clock is perfect
And so are you
See the love
That passes through
And let it severe
What remains to date
In a good way; never waver
it exists only if you know
How do you?
From scents
From sounds
And goals
And dreams
And more besides
But must one have a clock?

GOD IS ALL YOU EVER NEED

If bridges get burn
There is cleaning
If choirs sing
There is an ending
Life too has that
Like everything else
Admit it with life
Gone
There is still God
but without both
What do you have?
Some don't know him
Some once alive
Simple
They live, they do it
But if he is not in
Then what do you need?
One may have friends
Or those who say they are
Yet through the trials
There is one that holds your hands
Dries your tears
Comforts you soul
Raise one up beyond their imaginations
Beyond any friend's potential
The best friend one could ever have
The creator, always there
Most especially for eternity

WHAT OUR STORIES DO

Our stories hurt
borrow
Script writers minds
For a moment
They could

Our stories bring smiles
To faces
Or tears from good places
They rest in the hearts
of everyone, children,
men and women
Humanity awaits
Suddenly
it would

Our stories heal
Soothe
Bring solace
perhaps
They should

LOVE

Confusing
Crazy
For one in love
Learning pain, hurt, lasting love
coinciding with new beginnings
Letting go
Feeling renewed again
Or contemplating the birth
of sweet feelings

Overtime memories to last
Not forget
Loyal qualities to
Rehearse
Betrayal to omit
Maybe
Lies to ignore
unfolding and folding
Finding, researching,
how to love once more
sometimes

JUST EMPTINESS

All I see is nothing, all I hear is me, nothing
My heart bleeds, I seem to get blind with ease
But there is just emptiness, nothing
You were my everything, my heart and soul
My number one, my cavity, my blessing in disguise
You were mine, all of me

I have me now that you are gone
But my heart aches and that is
the emptiness that you left behind
My tears dry up on my cheeks,
it is like a watered flower bed
Yet the flowers can't blossom;
they are in fact unable to bloom
The seed just got interrupted
The hole remains

Just emptiness is all there is
The pain is now dull with no clarity
I feel nothing; nothing like flat ginger ale
Just emptiness; our story is at your grave

GOSSIPER

Cautious of nothing
or Something within
that fuels the fire of the drama he brings

You say, I say he says,
she says and they all say
And every little crippling thing
Will talk about and never to
Nor stand to see how it unfolds
But slander somehow willingly
Not listening to the stories told

In a little while the gossip flies
None catches it and it is usually
 mixed with or full of lies
Secretly believing and seeing dust
Only specifically while none
appears as mending tides
The crust of it may reveal some truth
But who knows what
how the bearer pays his dues

Whispers than start running wild
And no detective stands apart
Instead the gossiper never a nulls
the focus of the vicious role
He instead plays to tear down
walls that he didn't help build or
gates he didn't first open to close
But only with his mouth he carries
these loads and later

His hands say I told you so

He then feels he has accomplished
his goals and congratulates
himself, because for him
his dreams are limited and ends
where he started and nothing more

SUPERSIZE YOUR DREAMS

Now settling is a bit like hacking
You know the deal, the process
But choose illegally to perform a skill
And exhibit talent you know well

But be reminded that
hacking has it's penalties and notoriety
Not forgetting the so disturbing consequences
Turn that around to positivity
Supersize, indefinitely change
the entire mental state
For you and not just figuratively

From a different perspective
your skills and talents
Can be as you, magnificent
Far bigger than you with no
condescending priority

Supersize, the world of yours
The opportunities in it are not catastrophic
Nor placed here out of curiosity
But for our benefits
The peak is surely small
But enough for all it takes to conquer it

CLIMBING THE LADDER OF SUCCESS

Society has a part to play
In deeming it necessary
Many folks can relay their stories
Of the process of which it takes

Birds have wings they are connected to
They fly high and wide
Never touching the sky
But enough to see the world
To land where it is quite safe

The struggle is never over
Until their wings are pricked
Or broken or clipped
Or death partake

For many wings are not connected
They build their wings with God's favor
But get slinked, double crossed, scarred, abused
Misinterpreted and so much more in the process

So much so until the ladder may get slippery
They wither and accept it
Others build wings that become tools to succeed
To elevate themselves in spite of hatred, drama,
Diagnosis of Environment and many cactus's

They climb over fire burning without wood
Thorns without clues
Flaws without character, flees without dogs,
Surviving without truly living a life

And many other kinds of circumstances
only believing that
A ladder is indeed made for climbing
No matter what it is called and
in spite of many circumstances

IGNORANCE

This is a very harsh word
For those who don't know better
of the entire story
Nor are they expose to much
Those whose laughs define them
Or anger consumes them
And whose mockery of others
easily explains them

Those whose lack of exposure
exposes them or whose
Education denies them
Yeah, it is a very harsh word
One to be used lightly or abused slightly
Disturbs the journey of the ones that know better
Interrupts those who validate a far better point

Ignorance in itself is not an embarrassment
if applied honestly
As there is a level in each and every one of us
But exhibiting it constantly creates
a problem of the lack of some
sort of decency in some sort of way

Therefore there is in face a name calling
Calling of insignificant or less than
Or whatever adjective or box to be pushed in
Yet and still there is something or someone, a human
One who may interpret or find excuses for it

And live to ignore it
But for goodness' sake
Let it not be your desire to be the very next culprit
Consider this and remember it as well
it is still quite a harsh word

WHY THE BLAME?

Blaming once before
Never brought me a gain
Never brought me gleam
Nor many more wins

The blame is convenience
To take the fault and guilt from me
Whether I'm wrong or right
The blame colors me with an innocent light

The blame is my tissue that holds
my nostrils in place
My Kleenex, my comforter
Because what I blow out of them
I can never inhale back in

COMMON SENSE

They say we've got five senses
Enough to make us
walk tremble and swear
Break chairs, tables and
our human rights are like human birds

They say we got five senses
yet we all are very scared
Tricks can get painful
May we all not burn in hell

if we already have
Perhaps mercy will rise
Grace will be given to
The courage that lasts
Endurance's career was already a hat
And that my friend isn't to be exact

IN GOD'S NAME

In God's name what do you want from me
Love, hate and how it interplays?
In God's name what do you want more?
State of my mind in a State of rage?
In God's name what do you want from me?
For killing me you made a mistake
A mistake more than once
The twirl lake trail
In God's name we all can only pray
that in his name we all will be okay

THOUGHTS TO PONDER OVER

YOU CAN ACHIEVE, ONLY IF YOU BELIEVE

AKEN VIVIAN WARIEBI

FOR INSTANCE

For instance you fell off the ladder
Try again
You fell in the mud
Try again
The mud was all over you
Birds picked at you and dogs licked you
Try again

Lift up thyself once more
For instance you got it within you
To get up, rush it now
Take your time because

in that instance
The bulb came on
Bright shining as the sun
For instance life goes on
And you are still here
And have surpassed it
survived it and revived it
Those tries gained

Guess what?
With imperfection and all
You are up standing with all your weight
of a different kind at
a different place in a different space

LET THE TRUTH BE TOLD

There may be darkness around you
it surrounds you
it seeps through you and covers
you from head to toe
Believe it
let the truth be told, it is there

There is darkness around you
Fighting itself, lost in your bubble
Like caramel in a thread
Let it not engulf you, if you may
It could very well unfold you
Let the truth be told; it could become you

Darkness is upon you
And it is as snail
But never forget
Well, let me just say
Let the truth be told
One more time

Light, some light is way deep inside of you
find it and let that light resurrect you
To let the truth be told

NOTHING GUARANTEED

Nothing asked for
No kind of rain
Only the sun with the moon at the heel
Nothing granted not necessarily a hopeless dean
A living will, a deed to not kill nor be restrained

But a lot of surprises all over the place
Nothing worthy of your questions
Only answers that are not guaranteed

Respect is left with questions
Romance is but a name
Nothing expected
Noting against the rules
Just a good old fashioned
attitude with a serious brew

No need for anger, no love pretends
No Soda for the giver
No ring from a friend
So complicated; I don't understand

No testing for pick-up
No smiles to depend
No relaxation moment
No contraband

Envy lost a neighbor
From the sweetest hen
Nothing guaranteed
Simply a country with no end

For all the moviemakers
dislike that special saucepan
With junkie kind of loving
The singing has no end
Sex is in the living
No guarantee that life will ever end

OUT OF COURTESY

There is something called courtesy
But it is strictly for courteous people
Not those who don't believe in the concept
of it's commonness
The bad news is it just may not
be as common or accepting
As one may think, and overall, only those
who feel it's application is relevant, heed to believe

The rules out of it, I want to thank you for
Your level of application of all types of kindness
There is in fact one thing that is common about it though
it is so very universal and not quite adhered to
Some just don't see that yet

LIFE LESSONS

Life teaches us many lessons
Sometimes more than once
We may or may not pay attention,
Grasp the lessons or understand the sums
Life teaches us many lessons
Some are the main course
lessons within and without,
our expectations, our disappointments,
our role models, our definition of success,
our journey to it all in one chunk

Life teaches us many lessons
I call them desserts or better yet
Our friendships, our relationships,
our dreams, our goals
Life teaches us many lessons
Our hors-d'oeuvre are not left out
Our roadblocks, they are all like
Our main course at our dinner party
You see it is the conclusion of our passion and purpose

But unlike our literal dinner, in life
This part of life requires some thought
Some navigation, some struggle, some trials,
perhaps some force and persistence
Like hors-d'oeuvre at an actual meal it is created by a chef
and with our actual life that Chef is our creator

All of these make our journey tasteful or distasteful
A lot is based on our choices whether we realize it or not
Because in life's lessons, we are beings, it's value, it's worth

are on our calling
We are travelling into what in everything we discover and in so doing we
Find who we are if we want to and enhance what we always have been or give out
We are full course meal with what we ought to be or what we become
A full serving of life's lessons
We therefore have to recognize its value, it's worth on our calling

BEHAVIORS

There are all kinds of tensions to justify
Our motions
Our styles of doing things
To prevent or start a commotion

There are many explanations
to clarify the reasons
Believing or denying
Our own parts played in it

There are many situations
circumstances that presents confirmation
of who we are or are assumed to be no matter
Our explanations

FEELING OFF

The day cometh from yonder
And we journey not knowing what to expect
Nor the mystery intact, for all seasons, all phases

The day cometh from yonder
And we give it our best shot
That may not be that much to some
But to us that is all we have
for that day, for that moment

The day cometh
Always if tomorrow comes
we greet it purposefully
Perhaps lovingly, perhaps not
With questions and answers or not
feeling off some day or not

Finding the balance may be a struggle for some
A privilege for others within that there is
A stay-cation if that
The day cometh, it is never a flop

INTERPRETATION

What does our mind say?
To us, it changes it is supposed to evolve
Grow and not stand still nor be silent
it is supposed to change adapt, perhaps more?

What does our mind say?
For the pain we carry?
The way we cope, as we observe others here of late?
As if we are all perfect
And all clear on the chase?

What does our mind say?
Or better yet what is it saying to us? Always?
A beautiful place to store thoughts
To calm down, refer to, feel refreshed
to begin the journey of us by expressions

to begin again, hopefully pleasantly
But then it may tell us otherwise
As if it isn't a beautiful place
But where darkness is permitted
to reside unlike Payton place

LIFE

A beginning or an ending
A fair play
Some may say
Happy, sad where emotions run wild
Where limitations take their time
Expressively

A period of some kind of thing
Slowly building good or bad
Cultivating into so much or so little
Flexibility
Amazingly so, blessings flow

Peace is lost in catastrophe
Fear and ignorance dance at an irresistible place
Exposure allows for our denies
Causes are led to reason of or reflect injustices
Again it starts or ends a certain way
Softly or dramatically

But with or without contributions
With or without any kind of explanations
It is just simply "life"
We either survive or live,
maybe both but especially deal with it

HELP

Help is always an extension of oneself
It is bigger than you?
Bolder and an experience of kindness
Love and peace maybe included

Help is always a presentation of oneself
To another
To people or places or so
Eventually planting a seed as if one is out doors

Imagine if help did not exist
Where would the world be?
How would it have evolve?
Between you and me, and all of us?

The change, the evolution
The compassion, the empathy
The involvement of assistance
The principle

Asking sometimes may be intimidating
May appear as weakness
Or some sort of beneficial passion
To each of us to everyone the same

OUR VOICE

Having a voice is a blessing of sorts
When it is validated even more so
A kind of purpose to raise awareness
bringing attention to causes
A sort of confirmation of our beliefs
Being explored
Expressed, praised, or relate
Takes a journey of it's own, once out there
Not sealed
But accepted
Not silenced, nor rejected

Not quiet, but loud or peaceful and calm
Fully representing all of us
And feeding the hunger within ourselves
feeds of our curiosities
Anxieties and concerns
believing we too can stand on
Our feet with or without noise
on our happenings
on our own recognizance

hoping, claiming or denying
Furthering our calamities
Our interests, our conscience
Our voice is indeed powerful
An instrument of action, reaction,
focus, determination, change
silliness, foolishness and all that jazz
of losing ourselves, and gaining ourselves again

BEAUTY

Observed admired from afar
By whom and who defines it?
Outward verses inward
I can't deny one is very different from the other
But both or one may last just a little while

As I see beauty, I sigh
Wondering who is inside the masks?
Who prepares to explain?
Or exaggerate or are they societal lies?

we see it so differently and we believe it lasts
But who are we denying and what are we really saying?

If you and I are beautiful
In, is out the same?
it does take me to see you clean
Transparent or with codeine?

So beauty says and beauty does
But there is a lot of in betweens
So enjoy the journey while it
lasts or you could be defamed.

FIGHT RIGHT

    If we need to fight
Fight for the good not only in public
Not only in crowded streets
or crowded hallways
Nor before the masses
Fight also behind closed doors
Disturb the conscience of those
who ignore justice
Or compassion or courage

Fight in darkness
Bringing light from beneath
The bridges not just above it
But burning houses or cars or picket fences
Spells war, violence and insecurities
Produces jail time and other issues
far more problematic

Fight right for certain causes,
send the messages politely without rage,
Nor screams, nor with fire in your purses
you matter and we all do
Our lives are one-time parcels, very very temporary
Let your actions speak of the crisis with dignity,
Integrity and for God's sake
some foul play of common sense;
remember it comes naturally

JUST A FEW WORDS

Just a few words can say it all
so count them, weigh them before you declare them
Just a few words can win you the lottery
But not with money but with a listening ear
Just a few words can make one think
But think too much and you will sink
Just a few words from me to you
Sometimes that is all that is needed;
all that is necessary

ADJUST YOUR LENS

Before you judge, live and carry your own
Because you have issues and others do too
Before you misrepresent, think
it could be your name
Being put in the gutter
Your character smeared
Your integrity questioned
Before you deny
Accept the change
Adjust your lens
don't keep it always at the same space
Guess what?
that's how you grow
Before you run, embrace
Don't take advantage
Know like you, others have their stories
Like you, they're human
So be human and make mistakes
But as you travel on your journey and
Through your humanness, gather experiences
Believe that adjusting your lens
Creates a different story
Hopefully a positive one
that will keep you always adjusting
and believing change
Positive change is good and very very possible

I'M A BLESSED CHILD

Sometimes I have a sorry face
An ungrateful brat I am
And sometimes I complain so much
The devil actually wears his pants
backwards and still stands

Sometimes I sit and wonder
What would life be if I was out yonder?
At times, I ponder if out yonder is right here
where I am or further

Sometimes I please myself a bit
Not quitting when irate
But then again who stares
and Says I'm proud
in this big puddle?

At any rate and in any case
There is a reason for thunder
Because the blessings keep on rolling in
For that I feel great and flattered

If only I could appreciate all of God's
unselfish love he sends
Perhaps in my weak way I would realize that
I'm a blessed child
and not a big blunder

I must admit, I'm not perfect
Yet compare myself with others
too blind to see and feel how blessed I am
bad align with sculpture find me in respite rupture

Today I want to tell the world
What a blessed child I am
Because I see the light
And know how privilege I am
To be given breath and given love
and life in numbers

THE VALIDITY OF SILENCE

Protects and deceives
at the same time
Wisdom
Attracts and reflect at the same time
knowledge
Presents and detects
Experience
Expose and deny
Lessons
Save lives and kills it
Denial
is quite necessary?
Believe
Unites and divides
Trust
Assumes and misguides
Lead
Prevents and deflates
validates
In all this validation
Hurts become a common thread of unity
Threats unspoken words
Unheard
Feelings
Actions
Regrets
Friendships
Power
Superiority
Silence

BEING YOU

You are aware that you are YOU
Your style can't be hidden always
Nor your personality
Nor your, what do I call it Identity?
Well, you must feel what freedom is
Or what it may look like
But are you free to be you?

Individuality is not sin
Freedom to express yourself
May be offensive
Who says?
Well, surprise yourself
Once it is positive

Remember pain can be released
not just with negativity
allow you to be you, embrace, it!
Believe, accept it
Being you isn't a crime
But a privilege

An opportunity to impact
Not just impress
to reveal, not just expose
to believe, not just receive
to teach and learn at the same time
So grow, don't deter
relax, you'll be alright
Be you!

NAKED WITHOUT A MASK

I stand before you with no mask on my face
Naked, but not ashamed of that
Obviously it scares you those scars that I wear
Those wounds that I carry
Those wrinkles that I bare
I bear them proudly

Because it is a part of me, my history, my story
All of me is in them and they are in all of me
My scars are bitter sweet
but genuine truths of who I am not partially
But wholeheartedly
Not grudgingly you stare, yea I know
Just wondering why
I don't hide the scars that make me who I am?
The scars, you see present, as I am becoming a complete being?

I stand before you without a body mask either
You see me clearly hopefully
At least that is how I interpret that until I retire
Your questions and wonders and stares are puny little steps
But be grateful because I am real indeed
With the nerve to take my mask off
As I stand as vulnerable as can be

I stand before you so you can see
Being naked, barely says a word but says a lot
To those who want to hear
Those who choose to listen to my words unsaid
Those who not only stare but accept me fully for who I am

But a few would though
Because fakeness almost always gives the first impression
Diamonds rings to wear
And yes, I prefer no such notoriety
Because I stand naked not only for criticism
But to enlighten the new generation
That bareness isn't so bad after all

THE MIRROR

A reflection of you
A clear definition
A reminder of you
Clearly stated

If what you see is truly you
You see yourself completely or else
You're fooling you

If your view is the alternative
Make no mistake it is still a part of you
Just in case you didn't know
That mirror tells a bit of you
Or more besides maybe all of you that did not appear

Listen to the mirror's voice
Remember the message or perhaps a journey
On your hemisphere
What do you see, if I may ask?
The you, you know or someone else?
How do you embrace the image?
Or do you void the truth that it is telling you?

Never deny yourself the privilege of knowing you
A mirror isn't always there
Yet still remember the view that you are absorbing
Let it not make you over from who you thought you were or could be

But instead merge together, scaling out the old, worn out version

And bringing in the new that becomes you...
That is if the mirror doesn't quit, then neither can you

YOU ARE A REFLECTION OF YOUR FRIENDS

Who do you have in your circle?
Who do you associate with in your life?
Are your goals the same? Are your dreams similar?
Is there a familiarity in your personality?
Although that may not be necessary
But some things are common in actuality.

What is your purpose and what are theirs?
Ask yourself these questions if you dare.
If you do a wrong what is their reaction and
What is their advice upon request?

What if you do what is right?
Does it seem wrong or do they want a fight?
Look in the mirror from time to time
Do you see them looking back at you?

Are you proud or ashamed of that reflection?
Are you scared or do you feel safe from that reminder?
Please, think of those things.
Because not every friend is your friend

You may know that some are an enemy in disguise
Some want to see you fall hard and not fly high
So, if you see a different reflection than you can tolerate
Perhaps you need to think about it and try letting go
But first evaluate the reason for such a friendship.

THE BEAUTY STAINS

While young, vibrant, proud and true
Confusion takes in all
The confessions of few
But bearing our weight
We stand in our own way
With big heads from admirers, not few

The stain is on us fresh and clean
We're young, we're classy, we're petty or all three
They see our figures and sexiness reigns
We carry the "beauty Stains"

Annoying the jealous, the haters with fame
They wonder how come, we're not even tame
but with scented perfume and belonging to the right team
hmmm, we think we are validated with the beauty stain

Fancy, pretty, hot and attractive
Many people constantly call out our names
We then think it is okay to be popular and mean
With the cool and calm,
Promiscuity become slowly our favorite name
Only the stain wears off and so do we
Then wearing ourselves out
We are the crispy machine

IF ONLY IT WASN'T A LIE

Promises versus honesty
Integrity versus pride
if only truth could wear fine clothes
And lie the rags so old

Stories are told to be quite believable
Convincingly so but who knows?
The details beneath the surface?
Except the driver, the real source and God?

Fiction comes naturally for some
And they call it fantasy
And can't differentiate
Is that you or me or both of us?

Believing it all naturally
How credible is it if we don't ask?
For false seems far more acceptable
But deep inside after scaring away truth
We have regrets

And our conscience says, if only it wasn't a lie
That we've been told, but still embrace it as truth
Constantly knocks on our door wearing
the same clothes it always wore

THE SNORING SONG

Like a choir there is every tune imaginable
Very tune results from some sort of something tangible?
I suppose
Could be a song by one or many
Could be a duet from tireless subsiding

The music, if recorded produces a good laugh
But is truly quite annoying
for those who don't have an alibi
At times, grunting follows and
other noises in the loop
it starts slowly and the deeper
one sleeps the louder it carries

Awakens, disturbs, aggravates and
actually needs it's own directory
For reference, a conductor may be able
to participate as if conducting
a rehearsal tunes actually
But the deal is that
there is something to say for it
it is either leading to a diagnosis or
one is simply tired or stressed out
As if this is determined eventually

When treated or controlled, if
possible, there is a reason to celebrate
But for the record, wishful thinking is
all that is done for the disappearing act
or much better a victorious party is
if it is totally eliminated professionally

CELEBRATE LIFE

I celebrate Life, which is my choice
In order to have courage
A state of mind, I have
One of hopes not Pizzazz

I celebrate life, although
Sometimes I see and feel good and bad
The state of mind, I have
Is one of positive thinking

I celebrate life and this is my choice
I choose to walk on earth with a smile
Making a difference? For that I try

I celebrate life from all sides, every minute, every hour
All the good that this world has to offer
Every day as I live and survive, I celebrate it all and you?
Tell me, and you can feel free to cry

I celebrate life by choice
We both can cry, and laugh, and hug and smile
While building a bridge of possibilities and opportunities
With each of us celebrating it, with our very own style

SUPERIORITY

For the powers that be
This is the place for the powerless to know
And be reminded that they have no power

A place where those who don't know the value
of power take it for granted
A position where being or
feeling superior is supposed to be
A privilege or a way to possess
the power one never had

To be superior is for many
a rite of passage when they feel they have made it
Accomplished, or have some level of authority
You see, when a man has any amount of power
That's when one knows him most thoroughly

Even part of him comes out and
every side of him shows
To digress from what he wishes,
he is very slow
Power is sometimes necessary and
if used appropriately
Can work quite efficiently

it is good to remember like life
it is only temporary
When abuse or used at other's expense
Well, that is truly another and
quite an entirely different story

THE LIGHT IN YOU

Depending on you
other's work their weaknesses at your expense
Smile, it is a happy place
For your light to shine through

Others sabotage their happy place
Smile, they lack self-reconciliation
Some oppress, depress, or
traumatize you for attention
you're in the limelight

Smile and see light instead of darkness
Handle the light not the darkness in
your action or reaction
For the darkness can only destroy and
the light can always build a safer space

So let the best in you shine through
That is a blessing to all who cross your path
All who believe in you
Can see the good qualities you harbor
Never dim it, that light
Let it guide you through your journey, your path
From this a vision is born and other's too

INJUSTICE

It crowns it's head on everything
the good especially creating a kind of ugliness
That is hard to comprehend
Perhaps very difficult to articulate
Obviously it introduces a sort of pain
That is like a difficult pill to swallow

It is far beyond what we see as fair
An unfairness isn't a word used to describe it
Because it is not it's equal
It brings from us a hate that we didn't know we had
An anger that can swallow our pain as if it ever did

It crawls beneath our sense of self
As if ignoring as it passes by our peace within
It redefines our beliefs in systems
In humor of who it perpetrates
Who the victims are or seem to be
Who we choose to see and who we may blindly ignore

It interprets for us our own definition of self
And have us look in the mirror far more than
That sometimes hurting ourselves far more than
We ever did before or ever would again
We just can't seem to walk away
nor stand by idly

Or preach nonsense given to us years before
known as our history or our story
But...we must feel within us and in the process learn what peace is

We may never know the birth root of this type of hate
Although we may think we do, we must advocate peacefully
Quietly, silently for any other way is harm to us first
and not necessarily to anyone else

And no I would not condone it
But our actions will fully teach those
who choose to learn of our plight
our strength, our value and that we too are worth it?
Living this life, we live coping with it

TAP INTO YOUR POTENTIAL

Look beneath the surface
Without your eyes
Your heart will tell you
Where it lies
Seek refuge in the love of your being

Have mercy on you
For what you find may just surprise you
But delight and enlighten you
Tap into your potential

Your life awaits
You don't have to be quick
just thorough, not even slick
Fishing all the way
Your soul holds mystery

The good news is, it can be identified
And petrify your race
Indulge into the sweet nothings of you
Please ignore the negatives
Or recognize them at a slower pace

Your life needs you
it is waiting for you to do the tap
The drum can't beat without it
Your dance has no rhythm unless it
Taps into you or for now think about it

INFERIORITY

This is defined differently
to different people, for themselves
it may be imposed upon another
it's power is validated by the perpetrator
It teaches but, in the lesson,
let what is thought of has the less of you

Become the strength of you
That is where patience, tolerance,
 ignorance is processed
or generated if the less of
you is then all of you

Do you know love?
Love like pain and agony
has different levels
comes with various flaws
One thing is common to all
Standing Tall

Darkness looms between every oddness
Every narrow pathway
Films are made, some of disgrace
Some of honor, some of dignity
But do you know love or pain or agony?

Do you know what level of love you're in?
Or what level the law says is clean?
Do you know love?
Does your heart often bleeds?
Well, be equipped, prepared, focus, and rotate

Did I not say that you may have to adjust your sails?
If or if not consider the waves and the alternatives.

HATRED

Hatred never leads to anything good
But darkness, dirt and pain
I'll be satisfied when it is over
Drowned in hell where it belongs
Are we all willing to let go?
Or do we harbor it for future reference?

If love is so deep magical and pure
Why or why is hate so necessary?
Okay, so we ignore it?

All in silence as times permit
Only we are just as evil if we tolerate
We are a part of the problem as we observe and wait
We become the judges of our own cruel ways
and rise no higher than what conflicts make.
At times silently

START ANEW

This is about forgiveness not to anyone else
But oneself
Not to anyone who pretends,
shows deviousness, or deceit
Not to anyone else who is sure
he is great and sweet
And we all need forgiveness everyday
Definitely not half way
It starts from you and you alone
If you deny, don't blame the crowd
For you, like life, is breathed from up high
You have to understand that forgiveness
only keeps you in suspense but also helps
you become whole again.

SCARRED FOR LIFE

A lie can destroy many truths
That were evident or clear
It can ruin the future
And damage the present

It can debase you
And confuse you
Yes, really
It gets to that point

When one lies
A victim is born
Though we may move on
The scar remains

Usually comes from our circle
But use that scar and liberate you
Free yourself first and guess what?
In so doing, you can free the very ones that scarred you
And freedom in freedom is a win for all and you too!

THE COMMON THREAD OF HOPE

I hope; you hope; we hope
I believe it grows and spreads some more
like holding onto a grapevine planted in the dirt
or fighting to reconnect or striving to be the one blessed
The common thread it carries, the life it sheds, burns
The fog it clears, the needle it threads, the pain it removes

The burden it lifts, it is all worth it
Never denies pain, only soothes
And comfort is what it brings
Yet, and still as common as it is
Beyond the mere commonality of the thread
Far beneath any moment of despair
Hope lives within, and without
In spite of fear of the unknown frailties

TRUE CONFESSIONS

We confess the truth and the lie
And hope they buy it
Hope it sells
We confirm and convince ourselves
All the freaking time
while hiding behind our shadows
Where the evidence lies

We remind ourselves that life goes on
And the memories hold true
Today, tomorrow in every way
Only we try to avoid the naysayers as always

We profess to be what we aren't
Or remain what we are if we can
We think we should
We imagine we could
Truly our confessions and

Our stories are repeated constantly
Telling us that we're not alone
Nor ever will be, if we are true to us
Before anyone else, the lies disappear

ABSTINENCE

One never needs to protect themselves
Always protected, a sure thing
never taken for granted
But laughed at as goodness
sheds on an active sex life
Like a curse or a cure of promiscuity
Taken for granted
Shocking, depending on age range facilities
Furthermore, suffering an affirmation, a declaration
A piece of rare quality
Now or never acidity
Still existing far more than within our reality

THERE IS ALWAYS BETTER

What you have can be better
What you do can be also
Without the force of fame
Nor war, nor greed
Gradually with a steady pace
Focus

How you react can be better
Far better and it is called best
But best may change
Depending on the circumstance
Be determined

There can always be better
But exchanging better for worse well, I wonder
Blessings flow, songs are sang
Spiritually born, we are not declined, remember

There is always better, but who says?
Do you mind my better?
Just don't bury my best
you too can get there
Unisom

THE SONGS WE SING

Stupidity can be abused
like anything else, or used
so can intelligence, persistence,
power, and man

The songs we sing
We write everyday
As if to say, wait
Make sure the lyrics are great

Annoyance, fantasy, diamonds, and pearls
Remind me how our songs are made
By one or two or many of us
Waiting to exhale or die or
find our way in between

JUST SOME RANDOM THOUGHTS

BE CAREFUL WHO YOU SMILE WITH,
THEIR SMILE MIGHT BITE YOU

AKEN VIVIAN WARIEBI

SCARRED FOR LIFE

A lie can eventually be used in a way to scar one for life
It can destroy many truths that are
evident right before your eyes
It can totally destroy your future and your very present
It can dehumanize you, yes really,
it can get to that point and confuse you

A lie isn't the only type of thing that can
lead you to all kinds of abuse
There are many other forms
that can scar you for life and hide away the truth
Jealousy and hatred are just a few
Bullying is very much a part of these too

The scars remain; a victim is born
But yet and still we all move along
You may or may not have lots and lots of friends
Remember frenemies are in the same bunch
They all walk with you as you walk your journey's song

You can be scared for life in many ways
First and foremost, it usually comes from your circle
But use that scar and liberate you and many others
But free yourself first and guess what? In so doing,
You can free the very ones that scarred you
And freedom in freedom is a win for all and you too

WITHOUT A DOUBT

Without a doubt, I stand with God
In the beauty of his holiness
Surrounded by his grace and mercy
His courage, I hold so very dear
he speaks to my soul
His tender voice I hear

My heart listens keenly
As I carry on what he presents
To me from far and near
Like my life, what he gives is not for me alone
A pleasant burden to behold not just a present to unfold
But a blessing that blossoms from a seed that no one knows

Without a doubt, he holds me in his care
He knows my flow and how I stand
Amazingly, he prepares
He sees the unseen, an unknown classy stand
of which he takes me around the bend

No need to fret, complain, nor fear
No need to cry a bucket full of tears
Or climb a wall with misery in the air
Without a doubt, I know
he hears a simple prayer
from me his child from everywhere

IN LIFE...LIVE

Sadness can be placed on the back burner
Feelings of discouragement can do the same
Sometimes the closed door is for a reason
As they say, prevention is better than cure
And this is not treason
Crying is relieving; so is pain releasing

But I'm not saying the scar erases; I'm just saying that it is very important to stay sane
In life, live for the moment that is all you've got
Moments disappear, memories do not
Feelings come and go, and that is a fact

Some are situational
Some feelings fit that first row with locks
Live the moment; give it your best shot
Do what you can
You never know how that space, that time
Will nourish your sight and I betcha
It may make it grow a lot

So live life now and with no bad intentions
I say ask yourself; procrastinate if you may, and say why not?

NEVER CALL YOURSELF THAT

Never say the negatives to you
The opportunities may escape you,
This is not fair to you
You have no knife, but saying those things
Is like putting a knife right through you
Your heart fails and so do you
And yes, like life you have only one of that

Never pull yourself down
Even if the world tells you otherwise
You know you're far more than they
So excuse them for ignorance still lives

I'm dumb; I'm stupid; I can't; I'm lazy; and I'm a fool
I'm so much more than all of those
You see, erasing those, leaves room for the pleasant phrases
I'm smart; I'm gifted; I'm intelligent
Well, you get the picture

Imagine the beauty in you
Tell those beautiful words to you instead
Imagine, just imagine
How your head, your life, your love for self,
Your being would operate

FANTASIES

Coming clean or true no doubt
Coming from far or near
Or many other avenues that you can't imagine
The ugliness you feel as you
Doubt the clarity of your dream

Or the fixings on your opportunities
That settles on your lane
They hit you like a break wall
But your reality is not close
But if you can't figure out the road
you'll gently close the doors

To fantasize is nothing bad
It surely beats being bored and thrown outside
But actually so many times we leave it still wearing clothes

LISTENING

An important skill that many miss
Because they're anxious to reply
In many circumstances, they don't try
When the noise breaks
And the silence ticks
No one can sow nor hide
Because listening is a special skill
That puts the world on fire

Just think a minute and think real hard
The fools can't learn this game in a while
Because of the messages it brings
Are not for the sick and the very tired
Some try to send some crazy,
Play mind games or such

Their own flaws, they try to hide
By managing deceitful measures
Is how they crucify
A fool one has to be, to learn
For temporary slides, depending on the situation
None has to know who lied
But listening is so even with the ears and the eyes
Because the value of the sentence is when pride flies up high

SOME PEOPLE

Some people listen and learn some see and churn
Some wonder and dream some hear no fees
Some laugh through their pain
Some don't use their real names
Those "somes" are you and me

Some people have wrinkles and gray
Some spent life in dismay
Some live to blame and complain
Some live in their shadows all through life's way with shame
Some let greed reign supreme
Some further their studies and avoid the highways of fame
Some figure their bodies are some sort of diary to redeem
Some people just wait, while other's hesitate
Some touch lives, some destroy lives and some are irate
Some reverse their stories, by serving others with misery
Some smile hiding their hurts,
Others observe themselves in broad daylight

When darkness comes, life happens
But some turn on the light
Some people express kindness, in various ways
As if they know you and their story
Some gossip unsympathetically, admiring all your worries
Some people are just people who do all of this

But rest assure that all people depend on some people to make
or break their way through hell's gate
While heaven accepts all our stories
through life's process and offers
Forgiveness with empathy, pity also

Accepts also from sorrow, not hate to the death of our bodies
Nor the altar of regrets and yet, yes yet,
some people are just grateful hypocrites

FREEDOM...A QUESTIONABLE OFFENSE

Free from what and who to deny to rely
To recite speeches, perform protests, suspend folks who care
Clarification, of what changes or stays the same
How often do we preach against oppression
Prejudices and unfairness in public
But practice it on the side as a means of feeling
Supreme 'because superiority isn't to blame
For a practice of ignorance of a certain regime

Freedom of a questionable offense
Rises to every occasion so humanity claims
But with limitations, we barely refer to our own name's location
Or our vibration is misunderstood based on other's perception of
Our originalities and destinations but to question out of
frustration

Holding unto God's outstretched hands for consolation
For the journey seem to have just started the cries of generations
before us
Are heard not in anger but pleading that we remind those after us
That with freedom, we are burdened with our own bread
and can't be too comfortable with our skin
Or it could peel off, then where are we with dignity?

Who are we with solidarity and what are we other than humans?
So where does freedom begin and where does it end?
And really how free are we?

KIDS

One in a million kind of people
None the wiser
But words and actions often expressed
Makes for a raised eyebrow

Kids, they wear you out once in a while
They "kind of" sometimes lie
But referring back isn't their dreams
Just to let their way abide

Forsaking them, well I must say
The angels stand right by
And often they are rescued
When their innocence are portrayed out loud

The adults wonder why, when the shy ones get by
From pulling a wool over anyone's eyes
Especially the head of the crowd
Kids tell the truth in an honest way
With no filter

But when anger seeps in their mood one day
You'd be very surprised
Some are visionaries for tomorrow
Some try to read passersby
And then it seems amazing when
they change the entire world as they are

WITHOUT A THOUGHT

He did it without a thought
Because he loved me; from my head to my toe
With my flaws and my soul
He loves me

Without a thought, he forgives me
Reminds me of unconditional love
He spells it out like ABC
Makes it very simple for you and me
He teaches us, through each other
To do nothing but love one another

Without a thought, if we bend our knees
We talk with him like no other
When we fold our hands, we do the same
As that my friends, should also come naturally

We criticize crime and judge ourselves
We pretend to ourselves, that we are clean and fine
Each one thinks he is nice and kind
We feel safe in ourselves to whitewash the fines
He stands and smiles and forgives
Without a second thought in his mind

FINDING PEACE

Peacefully calming, life goes on
Without chaos, without height
Without force, like a wave that changed its mind in the ocean
Mapping a different course or a fire
that burns no more

Peacefully, the road is not shallow
Nor the water's edge not deep
Water flows in every corner
But with a marvelous control, the heart beats

Who creates the peace we seek?
Are we looking for a feast?
Mother nature never promised
Nor did we demand this from our weep

Finding peace is what kind of contentment?
We ignore the presence as we leap
Yet we stand like a carnation
For a pinned up vest, so neat

While we search and walk empty handed
God implanted without defeat
The peace so often we search for in our quest
For finding peace, he places it in us deep down within

LIFE'S LITTLE STORIES

Life's little stories, happy in unawares
When we don't know the whole story
Nor can figure out the rest
In lumps and all kinds of pieces
We give in with our best
Not knowing in our ignorance
The staring is then the worse?
Coincidences guide the pathway of many a rest

We walk on the journey blindly
Figuring out the tests
But life's little stories never begin without the answers first
But only with limited knowledge of what we do in depth

Yeah, life's little stories may not tell us as much
But bear in mind the journey remind you of many things
That will bring out your story, your work and your very best

Life's little stories start from birth, my friends
But one would never know it; not you at any stretch
Well, when the future comes and
When you twist and turn, and yell
You'll find that conclusion of the many lessons you've learned
So well, you'll exhale and you'll pitch yourself too much

So relax and feel and learn
On every step you take towards your life
Because life's little stories can make the big ones seemed rehearsed

THE MEETING PLACE

It is a pleasure
To meet those that I don't know
I know our path crosses for a reason
Why? We may never know
Indeed we can value our meet
Or take it for granted

We could embrace each other
Or shun our existence
Nonetheless, the moment is still a moment
Just for both of us
With or without regrets

We allow each other the space
To grow or remain stagnant
In our acquaintance
It is our choice
It is our pendant

YOUR SPARKLE

You have a sparkle, shine, it is there
The good news is you don't have to search for it
It is right before your eyes, right at your fingertips
It stares at you everyday, you ignore
It beckons you "see me"
You view the outside, it is within, touchable, teachable, and reachable

Yet you choose to look elsewhere,
you are too busy, too occupied
You search the world and can't find it,
you pray for it, God laughs
You preach to others as if you have found your little thing
That completes you, you act like you are the solution
You have all the answers, and
 if you don't feel that way and I'm wrong
You never even try to tap into your inner you,
nor your own potential

To feel and sense your talents and gifts,
your skills, your authenticity
Evaluate your own qualities,
you instead convince yourself that
It probably was never there,
and has never been there,
And never will be

But your greatness is there,
present always, you are so absent
If you continue to think that your sparkle is out there
You are dead wrong,

wrong if you believe that your sparkle
Is outside your boundaries,
because it is so present, it is a part of you
It is a gift, uniquely so, a combination of talents, love and hate
My friend it is what you are made off, and it consists of all of you,
Yep, it is all up in you

LISTEN TO YOURSELF

Listen to you for a change
To your heart, your vibes
Your voice, your understanding of you
Listen to your soul, your conscience level
Your level of prospective as well, must be considered.
And how it portrays you
While hearing God through and through
Listen to the details of you and your story

It can't be denied, nor pretended and don't be ashamed
Nor place it aside, blocking yourself out of your story
Be it lack of self-maintenance? Oh, but I'll let you decide
The lies you tell yourself come clear, so beware
Listen to your fantasies, your dreams, carefully
Your goals, gifts, ambitions? But yes, they may want to meet you

Listen to your language, the one your body speaks
Your circle may need recycling
At times, just to stay sane

And who is in your corner, pay attention
The two are not always the same
Listen to the messages of your life
Then from all of that, listen to your truth
Hear what it tells you, so greet you
Be acquainted with you

Simply enjoy the introduction
And as you evolve and grow

And as you let God rule and you're not confused
Try and live truly by it, in public too
Since you just met your best friend
To love, cherish, and live with for the rest of your life

SCENTS

Smells like the fragrance
of a certain perfume or cologne
Those scents you wear
in unseen places
Somewhere it oozes out like wild flowers
Or may be indescribable
I believe it, do you?

The scent of oak trees
Or dried leaves
of piece of burnt cloth
or old feet from unknown sources
Being absorbed by a few or more

Smells like money
old or new
Not yet spent
Fetched from a pen
or new material untouched
Smells nothing like a baby
yet a baby's odor is within
All over it

As roses stayed red so it does too
Galloping away like videos
On you tube

THE DIFFERENCE

There is a difference
in one's demeanor
Attitude or gratitude
and what follows after
Attitude of anger leads to no altitude
and what is created
Moving forward may be disaster

Attitude of peace, pleasantness
and contentment may result in gratitude
and what messages that sends out?
Gratitude for achievements
And what it says about us?
Gratitude of accomplishments?
And the lessons we learn in the journey

And I won't go any further
For somewhere in this may be
gratitude of negativity or ingratitude
hidden beneath somewhere
Along the lines come
some kind of healing
of knowing or revealing one's true self

Identifying and mostly
Acknowledging, ourselves
let's not forget validating too
The journey of the path we are on
Know the difference

A DIFFERENT KIND OF LOVE

A love that celebrates
Articulate feelings
And generate positivity
With an even flow

A love that praises
Uplifts never dehydrates
Good vibes, good intentions
Presenting good possibilities

A love that focuses on uplifting another
Cherishing and embracing another
The weakness, the shortcomings
All seem like treasures

A love that adapts the natural, the real,
Of the relationship, it grows in a healthy way
To foster togetherness that makes a blessed union
This is a different kind of love
Truly it glows

A love so kind, oh so free
A love with a special kind of ambience
A love so pure, so sincere and true
That kind that knows me so thoroughly

A different kind of love
One of loyalty and all things good
Where has it been all along?
Sitting lonely and alone, silently awaiting me

KNOW THYSELF

God knows what he made
What he created
What he molded
What he decided
He knows exactly how
He knows you
So, it is left with you to know thyself

If through your journey
Through your path
You meet a lot of people who are proud
Just stand aside and see yourself
And know the necessity of knowing yourself

If folks lie or frown or cry
Know a burden with each of us lie
So, know before anyone else
Who you are and are made to become
This will lead you to who you are truly meant to be

IF YOU CRY

If you cry, remember that tears too are temporary
They roll down your face and express joy or pain
If you cry, remember your heart is released
And your soul stands by watching
The emotions get replenished
No worries, tears are a form of release of expression
A kind of energy of it's own keeping you in touch with your feelings

If you cry, know tomorrow shall come again as you renew your lane
The sun will shine again in your eyes
You are sunshine my darling your sparkle begins
We all know it rains but a bright light is behind
Arrays from the sun with all raindrops,
Thunder or lightning come
Some to only clear the way for a better day, a safer tomorrow

Remember this, every star in the sky, has its own purpose
So does the moon and the sun
So, remember this, nothing is the same every day,
Things eventually change, as we know them
So, wipe your tears after sometime
And bring out your smile, your strength lies therein
For it has been there all the while

BE CONFIDENT

There will be naysayers, those who will judge
Those who will criticize
Those who will want to be like you
Those who will want to have what you have
Or what they think you have, those who will double cross you
Or try to destroy you in many ways
Such as destroying your reputation
For no apparent reason
Be clean, stay focus. Most of all be confident
Let anger stay a distance behind
As the moon is far from the sun
You'll be okay if and when you stay true to you
With confidence, class, integrity, peace, joy and happiness
Will walk in your shoes with you
Be gentle with life
And confident in style

WHERE YOU ARE

At the moment where you are
You were placed there for a reason
As a messenger ,a sort of orchestrator, a blessing
Your placement is for you to learn and know
If nothing else, or prosper or grow
Your blessings could be killed or born
In your future, it will show

Your actions or reactions will lead you to it
Your approach, your style and your guidance
God gave you that assignment
It just didn't happen
Your presence in that space was and is necessary
Perhaps a necessity

You are to be used by God
Only if you are willing to accept the role
Embracing your truth in the process
Finding your purpose, no matter how long
Of your pathway, your journey
The span of time is temporary

Know this, everyone doesn't
belong in every chapter of your life
In your life, see that as an exit or
an entrance to new beginnings or endings
to a far better place, a better state of mindset
A lighter weight to carry

HONESTY

Truth is seen as courageous
A lie, well, is accepted
Because many wear a mask
So, truth is unwelcomed, yet can't be denied

Telling the truth or hiding it may
Bring hatred to another
A level that may never be disguised
For it reveals the wear and tear of every crack
In every corner of the slide

One may seem foolish or unwise
To breathe truth for honesty, is to glaze like flies
Or as bees in search of honey that runs wild
But with God's touch we can rely
When knowledge stays and wisdom shys

But the wise may act as fools sometimes
Although by far the Lord allows
So being honest now becomes a sacrifice to some
Or a few lucky ones from the evil side

A MOMENT OF PEACE

Forsaking the sources that hatred brings
The different containers that brew from the pain
The moment of peace comes and
What a relief
To dwell in the quality of serendipity
A blissful moment

Defining peace has almost always been
A kind of rendition of those who seek no grief
But instead share a wealth of mercy and grace
As kindness allows and as kindness gives

A moment of peace, a moment of blessings
May not be without pain nor drama
But hopefully fewer messes
What do we live for if not for peace?
For war can never give us the solace we need

Oh peace, how awesome
Oh how fine, oh how delightful
When we do not resign,
To grow, to love, forgive and recharge
The second, the minute, the hour
Peace becomes mine
Never a blind sight but good feelings
Rippling away to the unsuspecting kinds
Yet staying behind to fertilize with time

IN LOVE WE TRUST

We may trust God's love
For ours can be tricky
Sometimes not reliable
At times fake and full of pretentious emotions
And weightless words
Of unintentional expressions and wavy love
So ungenuine, yet so transparent or
Of another sort
Could be real and deep and genuine
Or distorted for selfish possibilities
Relying on lies
Accepting that and waving goodbyes to sincerity
And the truth of ourselves
Believing wrong for right
Fake for real, drama for karma
War for peace
Fields of dreams disappear in the process
 We lose ourselves returning in vain finding nothing
In the love that was never there
And was never meant to be

I CANNOT BELIEVE YOU GOD

My journey to self-discovery was designed by you
Forgive me if I didn't think I should
Your creation of me, I take for granted
You wanted me on this journey for a reason
That was greatness made by you

Oh, how I wish I knew
My memory has never felt so good
I think of you and know in me
I carry a little bit of light from you

I cannot believe you God
From all the things you carry me through
The enormous and little blessings you've bestowed
And now I am beginning to understand
Why there is a distance between you and I
Yet an undeniable closeness

I must say this is true
Although I now believe I do
Because your blessings keep me renewed
So, just let me say a great thank you
As you ask me how do you do

I can only sigh and speak
Oh Lord, I just knew
For all that I have and all that I am
It might have been you

IN SOME WE TRUST

Be careful with the ones you trust
The ones who claim they know your every whereabouts
The ones you believe will never hurt you
Nor defy your love
Be careful with your deposits
As far as trust remember Jesus, his story

The closest to you may be a foe
The farthest of your heart can only guess how so?
All in your circle may not scare you
But know that some may not genuinely love you
In all you trust take heed
For those smiling faces that never smeared your name

Your vibes may tell you
The situation may confide you
Think of the meaning of trust as a clue
Or you'll be bare, trusting only fools
Your life would tell what clothes you wear
And the ones barely there
Then you will know to trust a few, Peace

FEARS

To the ignorant, we fear
And fear ignorance itself
To want knowledge, we do the same
We fear disasters, disappointments, and pains
We fear differences, although we have many similarities

We fear shame some come with pride or what would
energize our souls

We fear good, only because it conquers bad
We fear ourselves at times
And dodge from who we are
To fit in, to belong, or to be strong
We feel we must criticize, and harm and judge and hurt

We may fear all the rules that we don't abide
Somewhere inside we become silent to
Respect our tithes
But we neither know fear nor understand it
How it cripples our process of life by not a simple hi

It may denounce our path to success
As if our methods must be revised
Fear allows our true selves to hide
And gracefully take our awareness
To know whom is our high

THE BENEFITS

God didn't ask us for benefits
He gave it, when he made us
Nor did he want reimbursements
Of the creation of us
He, unlike us, loves unconditionally
This should teach us and show us through his word
But we love conditionally most times
When we love, with him love is so unconditional
 This we do just in case of backlash or liability with each other
Simply removing ourselves from a great human quality
That affects humanity, in ways that we cannot see
Nor understand, until tomorrow comes, if it does

KEEP HOPE ALIVE

In times like these hold unto hope
Hold onto your goals
Your dreams come through that
If and when God allows

Your future is attached
Though unseen, life never stops
Until your demise
Hold onto all that serves you right

Keep hope alive
And keep shining through
The more you do
The more you move
Eloquently, lovingly, just God and you

Keep hope alive
See this as true
A new way to follow
A great way to live
So never give up
Hold unto hope
Despite the odds, he sees you through

FABULOUSLY BEAUTIFUL TOO

With wooly hair laced with natural beads and locks
And clothes that seem made forever for kings and queens
With a walk that strides like royalty and a smile like breeze
Spelling kindness along the way with a great facial expression
With shining teeth, that glitters like diamond
Yes, my friend you are fabulously beautiful too

With eyes full of love and clear like crystal
From water only found in a stream full of richness
With silky words, and a body of gold
Showing much compassion taken to help mankind
Yes, my friend you are fabulously beautiful too

Look in the mirror, what do you see?
I am sure it is beauty that none can beat
It fits your personality, your size
It is size get on perfectly
Fit neatly like a body suit
Except that is authentically you

Never feel like you are not up to par
Not good enough, never enough
Yes, you are all that and more
Feel it in your soul because you are fabulously beautiful too

Your problems never went away
They are just hired with grace from above
But left beautiful scars of good character
Great minds and perhaps decency
They revealed the authentic you
Yes, my friend, you are fabulously beautiful too

Your heart knows and so do I
I am you see, fabulously beautiful too
Please know that all types of beauty are beautiful
Because it lasts and sits with those who appreciate it
Celebrating it for all eternity

BUBBLES

We are all living in our own bubble
Some so rich, they know poverty exists
But don't know poverty
Some so poor, they see money as the enemy
Some so mean, they transfer evil
that is built from their own adversity

Some see kindness as weakness
But to avoid getting burned
They learn to disappoint, some deceive others, lie and misrepresent
From misinterpretations to misunderstandings

Some have ways or find them
to manipulate or intimidate
Who they feel is weak,
So, with all the bubbles
That we grow in
Which bubble are you in?

Some are afraid of those who don't look like them
Nor act like them, oh for goodness's sake
Some reveal themselves falsely or accurately
While losing themselves and finding themselves later
Or not at all, some have and some have not

And some want while others need and so I ask again
Which bubble are you in?

WE MEET AGAIN

Our arrivals are not leavened
But we're in heaven
Sharing tears of joy
Putting hate aside
Feeling alright
Please to see each other again

Our deaths are not crystal care
Yes, we left the earth
Without our approval
Nor from the leaders of this century
And we were not in a hurry

We are ecstatic finding peace
But not halfway
Believing, trusting what the path would make
Rejoicing as if we are cake

But the earth still stands over yonder
Some won't make it, no one can fake it
The lives we had but now there is no duplicate
Our spirits simply mix

At another level, a meeting quite differently
Directly a crucial point
Just before our souls get judged
The earth awaits…

WE ALL MATTER

We all Matter, in spite of our stories,
our cultures, our religions, our queries
Despite our journeys, our histories,
our glories, our adversities
Whether blue, black, white or red,
no matter the race
Whether short, tall and
Whatever else we hold to ourselves
We all Matter

We can hold on to yesterday, if we choose
But today we must remember
Yes, today may have a future clue
Tomorrow still bears arms
of our fuses, not only to fools,
 but the guilty too
But the noises would annoy
as the causes confuse

We can hate but that hurts us
Primarily because if we did love ourselves
we won't choose it
Listen, we all matter,
no matter our class or
what the heck out status says or dictates
Society surely knows it
But sometimes regrets it

You know, sometimes it may be misleading.
Because assuming leads the game,

so, understand this
We must lead the fight,
Because the struggle has always been real
Or we should follow not
Just the causes' message
But be real in our actions as well,
They should come from the heart
and not from the garbage

We must live what we preach,
hypocritical innuendos, countless benefits
or worthless conveniences,
we must stand for the greater good
not the evils
We so often respect then be less
If we know we all matter,
We need to treat ourselves and others gently
Much kinder when no one is watching or looking
We must spread love
not just speak it without example
We must not be silenced to injustice of any kind and speak
Good of all in their absences especially
And their presence sincerely

We must not change our views or values
that change lives for the better
In order to fit in, quite a temporary fix for the pretentious abilities
We are cramped into
but adjust it for the betterment of humanity
We all matter so "them" versus "us" has to stop
and unity has to take it's place

Forgiveness, compassion, courage,
love, must increase and work with our common senses,
standing to protest and cursing our neighbors after doesn't count
Slandering or belittling included
at least that is what justice concluded
But for this moment think
if we believe we truly matter and we act it, that will be
All we must do, no protest needed,
none would be necessary, maybe we should try it

Because we all do matter, so let's face it
We have the solutions
So, the puzzle is or can be fixable
We have to believe, we all matter
That is the beginning of a resolution
If we don't trap it
If we do so, we better learn and quickly
Time, you see is watching and waiting
and life is sticking to it

UNFINISHED WORK

Let me check myself in a minute
This falling thing may balance me and
Then I can create all my dreams from
The falls and highs and lows of life.
Then whisper in the ears of my goals
To continue to flow, no matter what the tide
Or what cards life cut me and then falling
And finding my way becomes easier in the streets of life
And getting up becomes gold.
Catch me later only to soothe me
Or cheer me up or even maybe, pray
Or just maybe to warn me of the trials
I may face each time I fall
Each time I awaken deeper and
Believe in going at a higher level
And when you do, I am on my own
Still …but waiting to be caught in today's taste
Or and perhaps enduring in the journey and complexities of
Tomorrow's future.
Catching me now may delay or not capture
A process of growth that tomorrow
Needs to desperately control and yet unfold.
But later yes later will mold me to become bold
The way only living knows…and so it goes.
Since God doesn't wear man's clothes.

Personal Quotations from the Author (II)

- The world is a me thing, far more than ever before, it seems. Perhaps it can be a "we" or an "us' thing, instead of an "us versus them thing", I've got hope that God will shed his light continuously within "us" and "we" will be considered because it isn't ever about "I or me" but us. May God's love shine through us and unity prevails

- We all wear masks, some of us wear one and some of us several.

- Giving haters any amount of your time, to acknowledge any of their invitations to drama or what not is allowing them to steal not only your joy, but you, wholeheartedly, refuse
 It is better to love any day!

- Silence is golden, so is communication diamond?

- Everyone has an opinion, whether you agree with them or not. Validation is quite necessary and if you think I am lying get on social media and you will soon see, feel and even express your own.

- Sometimes listening to our own trauma, no matter the size or level, teaches us and we learn and discard and that is a major part of our growth!

- Emulate only, yes only, the one who died for you by living and dying based on unconditional love, the love he has for you.

- The best thing that you can do for yourself and as a servant of God is to love and forgive yourself, as well as, showing it sincerely to your enemies... because that is what we all need the most.

- Listening to yourself could be the beginning of self-love and self-maintenance... so listen, do you hear anything? But in doing so don't forget God.

- When you love yourself completely, there is just no room for hate, your love spills out to the world

- There is a difference in being humble and being stupid, there is a difference in being kind and being weak, there is a difference in being smart and getting over on people. One portrays earned integrity and respect in the building of one's own character, the other does not. Please... know the difference and don't get it twisted.

- Unwrap the good of that which is hidden inside of you, it brings out the best in you never the worse, that is your gift to give to the world!

- God knows the timing... you need not worry.

- Today is another day with another chance to live, let's not forget the privilege to be chosen to do so

NOTES

www.ingramcontent.com/pod-product-compliance
Lightning Source LLC
Chambersburg PA
CBHW070554160426
43199CB00014B/2502